T0104347

Save the
Tigers

THIS EDITION
Editorial Management by Oriel Square
Produced for DK by WonderLab Group LLC
Jennifer Emmett, Erica Green, Kate Hale, *Founders*

Editors Grace Hill Smith, Libby Romero, Maya Myers, Michaela Weglinski;
Photography Editors Kelley Miller, Annette Kiesow, Nicole DiMella; **Managing Editor** Rachel Houghton;
Designers Project Design Company; **Researcher** Michelle Harris; **Copy Editor** Lori Merritt;
Indexer Connie Binder; **Proofreader** Larry Shea; **Reading Specialist** Dr. Jennifer Albro;
Curriculum Specialist Elaine Larson

Published in the United States by DK Publishing
1745 Broadway, 20th Floor, New York, NY 10019

Copyright © 2023 Dorling Kindersley Limited
DK, a Division of Penguin Random House LLC
23 24 25 26 10 9 8 7 6 5 4 3 2 1
001–334027–Oct/2023

A catalog record for this book
is available from the Library of Congress.
HC ISBN: 978-0-7440-7477-2
PB ISBN: 978-0-7440-7479-6

DK books are available at special discounts when purchased in bulk for sales promotions, premiums,
fundraising, or educational use. For details, contact: DK Publishing Special Markets,
1745 Broadway, 20th Floor, New York, NY 10019
SpecialSales@dk.com

Printed and bound in China

The publisher would like to thank the following for their kind permission to reproduce their images:
a=above; c=center; b=below; l=left; r=right; t=top; b/g=background

Dreamstime.com: tpʲn Kʲpl 18bl, Appfind 11b, Sergey Bogdanov 15tr, 19b, Arnab Bose 13bl, Vladimir Cech 12bl, 30–31,
Henner Damke 23clb, Sanjaykumar Daramwar 20–21, Donyanedomam 13tl, Ondej Prosick 6bl, 6–7, Vikas Garg 29br,
Jan Hejda 17br, Isselee 3, 14bl, 14br, 27cra, Kksteven 22cl, Martin Mecnarowski 23cla, Misad 17cla, Neil Burton / Natureimmortal
13cra, Petrsalinger 22tl, Riverrail 9t, Scheriton 22bl, Suriya007 12cr, Tomonishi 9bl, Anke Van Wyk 18tl; **Fotolia:** Eric Isselee 1;
Getty Images: Karim SAHIB / AFP 26–27, Dhana Kencana / Anadolu Agency 24–25, Enrique Ramos Lpez / EyeEm 8crb,
Thierry Falise / LightRocket 21cr, Win McNamee / Staff 28bl, Moment Open / Todd Ryburn Photography 29tr, Photographer's
Choice RF / Ronald Wittek 15br, Stone / Anup Shah 25br, The Image Bank / Martin Harvey 28crb;
Getty Images / iStock: ANDREYGUDKOV 10b, leezsnow 29tl, Tammi Mild 29cl, Photocech 16–17t; **naturepl.com:** Andy Rouse 4–5;
Shutterstock.com: Eric Isselee 32b, mihirjoshi 8b

Cover images: *Front:* **Getty Images:** The Image Bank / James Warwick

All other images © Dorling Kindersley
For more information see: www.dkimages.com

For the curious
www.dk.com

Save the Tigers

Ruth A. Musgrave

Contents

Meet the Tigers

Tigers are the biggest cats in the world. They are also the only big cats with stripes!

These strong and powerful cats live in jungles, grasslands, and deserts.

Some tigers live where it is cold and dry, and others live where it is hot and swampy.

Suited for Snow

Amur tigers live in the snow. Thick fur keeps them warm and dry.

Sizing Up Tigers

From nose to tail, a tiger is as long as two bicycles in a row.

Slight differences in size and fur color help them survive in their homes.

Tigers' orange-and-black stripes help these big cats hide as they stalk their prey.

Their colors and stripes blend in with light and shadows.

That makes these cats harder to see.

One of a Kind

No two tigers have the exact same markings.

whiskers

Tigers have whiskers all over their body. Whiskers work like an alarm to send messages to the tiger's brain. They help the cats find their way at night and know when to grab prey.

Long Whiskers

The whiskers on a tiger's face are longer than a child's hand.

Tigers use their sharp front teeth and long, curved claws to grab and hold on to food. Their back teeth work like knives to cut into meat. Tigers have the largest teeth of all the big cats. Both their claws and their sharp front teeth, called canines, are as long as a child's middle finger.

A tiger's rough tongue helps scrape meat off bones.
Cats also use their tongue to clean their fur.

Water Break

Tigers are good swimmers. They cool down and sometimes even hunt in the water.

Tigers' Prey

These powerful hunters only eat meat. They eat about once a week. Tigers hunt many kinds of large animals.
Here are a few.

deer

Asian wild dog

monkey

wild boar

buffalo

Little Tigers

The tiger cub hides in the tall grass. It watches for any movement up ahead.

Pounce! The cub catches its mother's tail.

Young tigers practice the hunting skills they'll need when they grow up.

Ready to Hunt

Cubs start hunting with their mother at about six months old.

They do this by playing. The cubs wrestle, chase, stalk, and bite their mother and each other. They catch flying insects.

Mother tigers feed their cubs until the young cats are old enough to hunt on their own.

Cubs also learn to hunt by watching their mother.

They stay hidden and safe, but they keep a close eye on her. She is teaching them how to survive.

The mother tiger walks quietly. She looks and listens.

Hear That?

Tigers rotate their ears to help zero in on the sounds of their prey.

She crouches down in the brush to watch a herd of deer.

Finally, a single deer wanders past.

The big cat pounces. She leaps two car lengths to catch the prey.

Hear Me Roar

An adult tiger's roar can be heard a long way away.

Roar! The mother tiger calls to her cubs. Time to eat. The cubs scamper out from their hiding place.

ROAR!

Chuff. Chuff.

They greet their mother.
Now it's time for a family meal.

Mom Time

A tiger mother raises the cubs alone. Cubs stay with her until they are about two years old.

Sharing Space

Tigers need a lot of room to roam. They need large animals to eat. Tigers and people compete for food and space.

Roads, farms, towns, and cities have replaced the tigers' homes. Many of the animals the tigers hunt are gone, too.

Tigers can be dangerous for people. People can be dangerous for tigers, too.

Finding ways to live near each other can be challenging.

Hunted Down

People hunt tigers for their fur and teeth and to keep tigers away from their farm animals.

Saving Tigers

Amur Tiger
Distribution:
Russian Far East and
northeastern China

Malayan Tiger
Distribution:
Peninsular Malaysia

Sumatran Tiger
Distribution:
Sumatra

The number of tigers is getting bigger in some places. But in most places, their numbers are getting smaller.

Bengal Tiger
Distribution:
Indian sub-continent

Tigers in Trouble

All tigers are endangered or critically endangered. That means that populations in the wild are so small that tigers could become extinct, or be gone forever.

Northern Indochinese Tiger
Distribution:
Indochina north of the Malayan Peninsula

How can we save the tigers?

Scientists and other people who love tigers work together.

They study the tigers in the wild and at zoos.

They learn more about these big cats.

Counting Tigers

Today, fewer than 4,000 adult tigers survive in the wild.

When people get to see tigers up close, they want to help protect these big cats.

Many tiger babies are born in zoos. The cubs at the zoo chase and play.

Growing Fast

A six-month-old cub can weigh as much as two seven-year-old children.

People take pictures and cheer for the cubs.

They fall in love with the babies and their mom.

Cute Cubs
A female tiger gives birth to up to seven cubs.

People work to make room for nature reserves. These are large places for tigers to live.

Reserves protect the tigers and their food.

Today, scientists know a lot about what tigers need to survive. People will keep working together to help protect these big cats.

Glossary

Big cats
Large wild cats, including tigers, lions, leopards, snow leopards, jaguars, cougars, and cheetahs

Endangered
Animals at risk of becoming extinct because there are so few left

Extinct
When a plant or animal group is gone forever

Predator
An animal that hunts and eats other animals

Prey
Animals that are eaten by predators

Index

Quiz

Answer the questions to see what you have learned. Check your answers in the key below.

1. Where do tigers live?

2. What helps a tiger hide?

3. How do cubs practice hunting?

4. How does the mother tiger call her cubs?

5. How do nature reserves help tigers?

1. Jungles, grasslands, and deserts 2. The colors and patterns of the tiger's fur 3. They play 4. She roars 5. They provide homes and food for the tigers